EXPLORATIONS

This book is proudly dedicated to Andy Duckett,
in recognition of all the pianos and lessons with which he provided me as

Richard Duckett

After winning the Cassell's Prize at the Royal Military School of Music, Kneller Hall, Richard went on to study music at the Guildhall School of Music and Drama. He has played extensively as a freelance hornist and has held various teaching posts, including Curriculum Co-ordinator for the City of Birmingham Music Service. Author of the popular 'Team' Brass, Woodwind and Strings tutor books, Richard continues to write and teach music.

Gary J. Price

After graduating from the University of Birmingham with an MA degree in musicology, Gary joined Birmingham Music Service as a peripatetic music teacher. He has since worked as a secondary music teacher, a primary music co-ordinator, and a curriculum support teacher for a number of schools in the midlands. Gary was formerly Head of Woodwind for Solihull Music Service, and is currently Head of Music at Queensbridge Secondary School in Birmingham.

Paul Slater

After graduating from the London College of Music, Paul toured France with a French Rock group as a keyboard player. He then started as a classroom music teacher but later became a peripatetic keyboard specialist. At present Paul is Head of Percussion and Allied Studies for the City of Birmingham Music Service, while continuing to compose and record.

SERIES AUTHORS	Richard Duckett and Gary J. Price
CD TRACKS COMPOSER	Paul Slater, Head of Percussion and Allied Studies, City of Birmingham Music Service
TYPESETTING AND GRAPHICS	Ed Duckett / Maria Jose Granda Isabel
COVER DESIGN	Phil Duckett
PRODUCTION	Ed Duckett

Sincere thanks are extended to:-

Cormac Loane	Head of Professional Development, City of Birmingham Music Service
Tonia Price	Instrumental Teacher, City of Birmingham Music Service
Joyce Rothschild	Inspector for Music and Drama, Solihull MBC
Trevor Jones	Instrumental Manager, Staffordshire Performing Arts
Louise Jones	Head of Woodwind, Dudley Performing Arts
Robert Vivian	Central Ensembles Co-ordinator, City of Birmingham Music Service
Roy Smith	
Jenny Smith	Strings Editor
James Cunningham	Instrumental Teacher, City of Birmingham Music Service

TWM would like to thank:-

Derek Andrews	www.futurenet-designs.com
Paul Gardner	
COVER IMAGE	Material created with support from AURA/STScI under NASA contract NAS5-26555
PUBLISHED BY	Team World Music Ltd 2 Reed Mace Drive Bromsgrove Worcestershire B61 0UJ UK +44 (0) 1527 835 878 www.music-tutor.net
COPYRIGHT	© Copyright 2003/2005 by Team World Music Ltd All rights reserved. No part of this book or CD may be reproduced in any form without written permission from the publisher.
REFERENCE	EXPLORATIONS Piano/Keyboard book + CD *Students' Edition*, Order Ref: TWM00149
ISBN	1-904776-00-0

Contents

Introduction

General Introduction

Explorations is a series of unique, practical workbooks of musical starting points for creative instrumental teaching and learning. It forms a valuable resource bank of progressive activities to aid the development of general musicianship.

Explorations is suitable for both individual and group tuition, for use both in school and at home. It has been designed to complement the traditional tutor-book. It is not intended, however, to be studied from beginning to end; rather, teachers can select activities to meet the needs of the individual student.

Each page in *Explorations* introduces one or more open-ended musical activities, offering opportunities for a variety of creative work. Central to every activity is the learning or refining of a key musical skill, such as improvising, composing or playing 'by ear'. These are presented progressively throughout.

Through *Explorations* students explore a variety of styles and learn how to create music in non-western and contemporary idioms. They are given opportunities to improvise and make music using the scales and modes of Indian, Japanese and Folk traditions and can also experiment with more modern sounds from the worlds of Blues, Jazz, Minimalism and Serialism.

Using the CD

Explorations comes with a 75-track backing CD. Many of the activities have backing tracks which aid learning during the lesson and practice at home. CD tracks are listed in the text as *[CD01]* etc. Some activities have more than one backing track, giving students appropriate accompaniment to support the different stages in the learning of the activity. Such activities include backing tracks at different tempi, tracks with model improvisations, additional tracks with scope for student input; or tracks which offer different interpretations of the same material. Every track is preceeded by a 2-bar introduction.

Using the Piano/ Keyboard edition

This edition integrates fully with *Explorations* for classroom percussion, recorder, classroom band and wind band/orchestra. As it is part of a complete series incorporating all instruments, *Explorations* for piano/keyboard begins with a G major tonality rather than the more usual C. However, pages 45 and 46 offer C major related activities which may be introduced to students prior to commencing the main course. Added to this, there are many activities in the first part of the book which can be completed in the 'C' position, e.g. Pulse Grids (p.4), Pitch by Steps and Leaps (p.8), Create-a-Chord (p.12), Dot-Dash Phrases (p.13), and so on. In total there are 18 activities suitable for playing in the 'C' position.
Throughout the book, chord symbols are provided relating to the keyboard's integral chordal accompaniment. These can be used in place of left-hand accompaniments, if required. If keyboards are used in mixed ensembles of more than, say, ten, it is strongly recommended that they are amplified.

National Curriculum Music (UK)

The activities in *Explorations* can be used to fulfil many of the requirements of the National Curriculum for music. There are links to music at Key Stages 2 and 3 and many activities can be used to develop skills for GCSE music.

Support from Team World Music Ltd

A list of retailers is available at www.music-tutor.net. Support and information on Team World Music material is also available.

Photocopying

Teachers and students can ensure that *Explorations* stays in print by not photocopying or reproducing any part of the publication.

CD Contents

Page	Title	Track	Total Bars	Description
4	Pulse Grids	01	[16]	Rhythm accompaniment at ♩=90
		02	[16]	Rhythm accompaniment at ♩=105
		03	[16]	Rhythm accompaniment at ♩=120
5	One-Note Rhythm Games	04	[32]	Eight example 2-bar phrases for copying or answering
		05	[32]	Accompaniment for improvising 2-bar phrases
6	Listen and Copy	06	[32]	Eight example 2-bar phrases for copying
		07	[32]	Accompaniment for improvising and copying 2-bar phrases
7	Listen and Answer	08	[32]	Eight example 2-bar phrases for answering
		07	[32]	Accompaniment for improvising and answering 2-bar phrases
9	Play a Well-Known Tune 'By Ear'	09	[8]	Performance of *Au Clair de la Lune* for listening and pitch discrimination
		10	[8]	First 2 bars of *Au Clair de la Lune* followed by accompaniment for melody to be completed
		11	[8]	Accompaniment for performing *Au Clair de la Lune* 'by ear'
		12	[8]	Performance of *Merrily We Roll Along* for listening and pitch discrimination
		13	[8]	First 2 bars of *Merrily We Roll Along* followed by accompaniment for melody to be completed
		14	[8]	Accompaniment for performing *Merrily We Roll Along* 'by ear'
10	Word-Rhythms	15	[16]	Performance of *Word-Rhythms* for practising clapping, saying-aloud, playing, etc.
		16	[32]	Performance of *Word-Rhythms* for practising playing/using notes in chord
11	Rhythm Grids	17	[32]	Accompaniment for *Rhythm Grids* using notes from the chord boxes
12	Staccato Starter	18	[16]	Accompaniment for *Staccato Starter* using notes from the chord
14	A Rhythm Round	19	[44]	Accompaniment for *A Rhythm Round* using notes from the chord boxes
16	Jazz on 3 Notes	20	[12]	Play-along performance of *Blue Triangle*
		21	[24]	Five example 2- and 4-bar phrases for copying or answering
		22	[60]	Two performances of *Blue Triangle*, followed by two 12-bar blues sequences for improvisation, then a final performance of the theme
18	Listen, Copy and Answer (1)	23	[32]	Eight example 2-bar phrases in $\frac{2}{4}$ for copying and answering
		24	[32]	Accompaniment for improvising and copying 2-bar phrases in $\frac{2}{4}$
		25	[32]	Eight example 2-bar phrases in for copying and answering $\frac{3}{4}$
		26	[32]	Accompaniment for improvising and copying 2-bar phrases in $\frac{3}{4}$
20	Name that Tune	27	[12]	Performance of *Twinkle Star* for listening and pitch discrimination
		28	[12]	First 2 bars of *Twinkle Star* followed by accompaniment for melody to be completed
		29	[12]	Accompaniment for performing *Twinkle Star* 'by ear'
		30	[16]	Performance of *Old Mac* for listening and pitch discrimination
		31	[16]	First 2 bars of *Old Mac* followed by accompaniment for melody to be completed
		32	[16]	Accompaniment for performing *Old Mac* 'by ear'
21	Instant Ensemble	33	[32]	Eight example 2-bar phrases for copying and answering
		34	[32]	Accompaniment for improvising 2-bar phrases
22	Rhythmic Decoration	35	[16]	Play-along performance of *Old MacDonald*
		36	[16]	First 2 bars of *Old MacDonald* followed by accompaniment for decoration with <u>repeated notes</u>
		37	[16]	First 2 bars of *Old MacDonald* followed by accompaniment for decoration with <u>jazz rhythms</u>
		38	[16]	First 2 bars of *Old MacDonald* followed by accompaniment for <u>decorating long notes</u>
		39	[32]	First 4 bars of *Old MacDonald* followed by accompaniment for performing in $\frac{3}{4}$

Page	Title	Track	Total Bars	Description
23	Melodic Decoration	35	[16]	Play-along performance of *Old MacDonald*
		40	[16]	First 2 bars of *Old MacDonald* followed by accompaniment for decoration with <u>raised pitch</u>
		41	[16]	First 2 bars of *Old MacDonald* followed by accompaniment for decoration with <u>lowered pitch</u>
		42	[16]	First 2 bars of *Old MacDonald* followed by accompaniment for decoration with <u>flattened 3rd and 6th</u>
		43	[16]	First 2 bars of *Old MacDonald* followed by accompaniment for <u>rhythmic or melodic decoration</u>
25	Chinese Music	44	[32]	Play-along performance of *Red Dragon*
		45	[32]	Six example 2- and 4-bar phrases for copying or answering
		46	[96]	Accompaniment (in three 32-bar sections accompanied by gong) for performing *Red Dragon*
28	Caribbean Rhythm Round	47	[22]	Play-along performance of *Caribbean Rhythm Round* on percussion
		48	[22]	Play-along performance of *Caribbean Rhythm Round* using notes from the chord boxes
29	Blues Booster	49	[12]	Play-along performance of *Movin' On*
		50	[24]	Four example 2- and 4-bar phrases for copying and answering
		51	[60]	Two performances of *Movin' On*, followed by two 12-bar blues sequences for improvisation, then a final performance of the theme
31	Whole-Tone Improvising	52	[16]	Two 4-bar, whole-tone phrases each followed by a 4-bar slot for improvisation
		53	[16]	Accompaniment for improvising patterns based on the whole-tone scale
		54	[32]	Atmospheric accompaniment for improvising/composing a 'spooky' piece of music
33	Listen, Copy and Answer (2)	55	[32]	Play-along performance of *Echo Mountain* (twice through)
		56	[16]	Play-along performance of *Echo Mountain* with 2nd part included
		57	[16]	Play-along performance of *Echo Mountain* with six slots for improvising answers
37	Salsa Rhythm Round	58	[44]	Play-along performance of *Salsa Rhythm Round* on percussion
		59	[44]	Play-along performance of *Salsa Rhythm Round* using notes from the chord boxes, at ♩=106
		60	[44]	As track 59 at ♩=127
		61	[44]	As track 59 at ♩=142
38	Dorian Jazz	62	[25]	Play-along performance of *Five Spice Jazz* (with repeat after DC)
		63	[25]	As track 62 with example rhythmic variation (for 5 bars only)
		64	[75]	Performance of *Five Spice Jazz*, followed by five 5-bar blues sequences for improvisation, then a final performance of the theme
40	Japanese Music	65	[14]	Play-along performance of *Sakura*
		66	[14]	Three example 2-bar phrases for answering
		67	[28]	Accompaniment for performing *Sakura* and improvising on theme
41	Minimalism	68	[34]	Play-along performance of given ostinati
42	Dodecaphonic Music	69	[48]	Play-along performance of tone-row, ostinato and improvisations
43	Improvising with Ragas	70	[16]	Play-along performance of *Raga*
		71	[16]	Four example 2-bar phrases for copying and answering
44	Jigs and Reels	72	[16]	Play-along performance of *Emerald Isle*
		73	[16]	As track 72 with rhythmic and melodic decoration
		74	[16]	Accompaniment for improvising in folk style
		75	[48]	Performance of *Emerald Isle*, followed by 16-bar sequence for improvisation, then a final performance of *Emerald Isle*

Pulse Grids

EXPLORATIONS

- These pulse grids, for one or more players, can be clapped, sung, or played in any position.
- Starting with the first grid, play each row from left to right, maintaining a 4-beat pulse throughout. *[CD01, CD02, CD03]*
- Then play the grid in different ways, for example, in unison, in harmony, and in rounds.

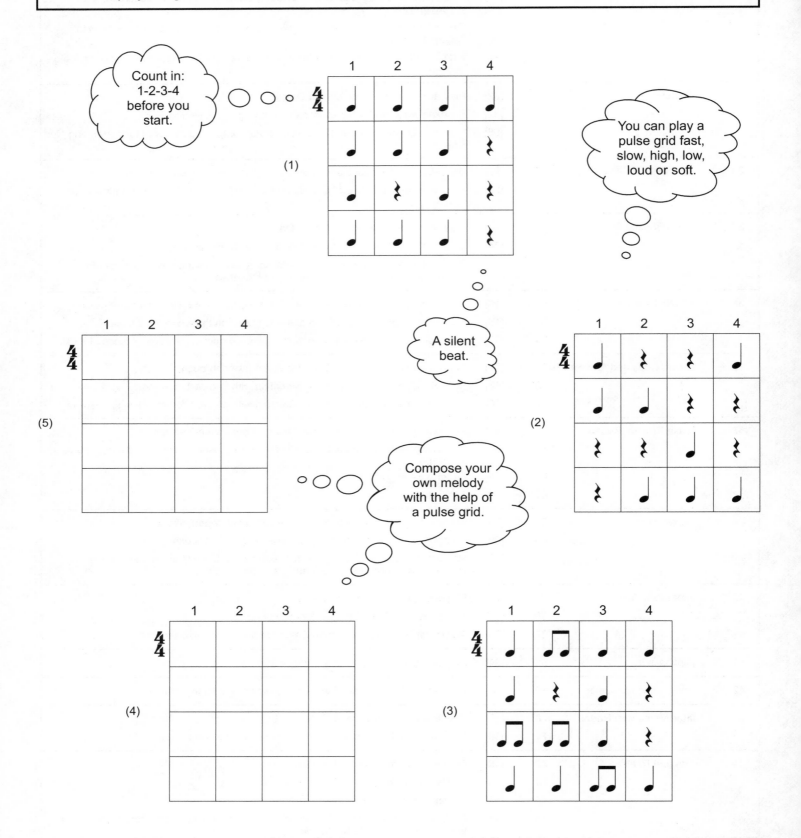

TWM00149

One-Note Rhythm Games

EXPLORATIONS

- These one-note activities, for two or more players, are example prompts for extended rhythm work and general musicianship. They can be completed with hands separately or hands together.

- In Activity 1, one player thinks of a popular tune and plays its rhythm on one note. The other player(s) must then name it and play it.

- In Activity 2, one player plays a 2-bar phrase on one note, and the other(s) immediately copy. *[CD04, CD05]*

- In Activity 3, one player plays a 2-bar phrase on one note and another player immediately plays a 2-bar answering phrase. *[CD04, CD05]*

- A 4-beat pulse should be maintained through Activities 2 and 3.

ACTIVITY 1

(Answer: 'Jingle Bells')

(etc)

ACTIVITY 2

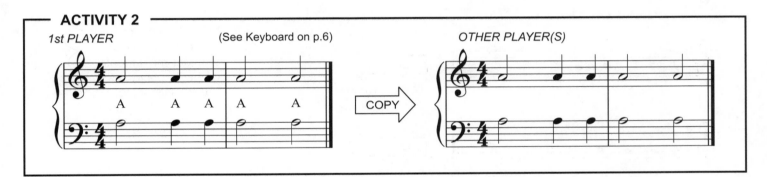

ACTIVITY 3

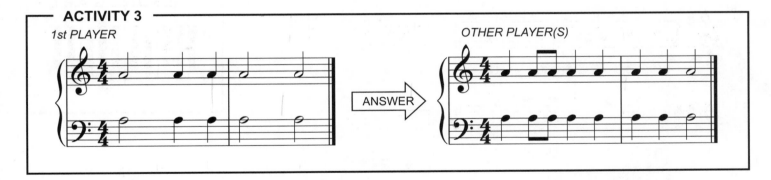

TEACHERS' KEYBOARD ACCOMPANIMENT (ACTIVITIES 2&3)

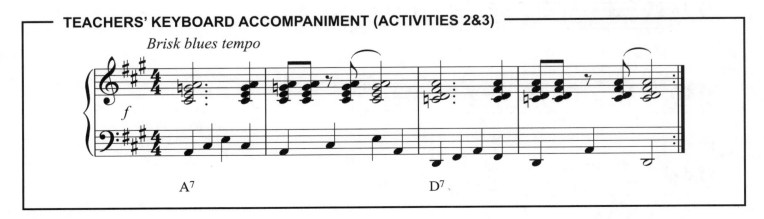

Listen and Copy

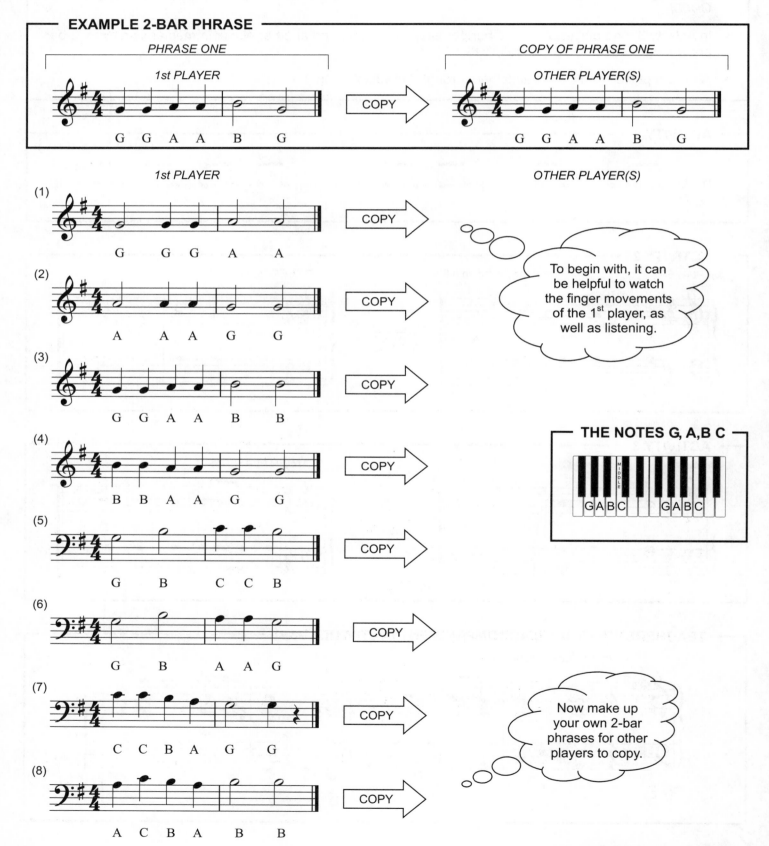

TWM00149
© Team World Music Ltd 2005

Listen and Answer

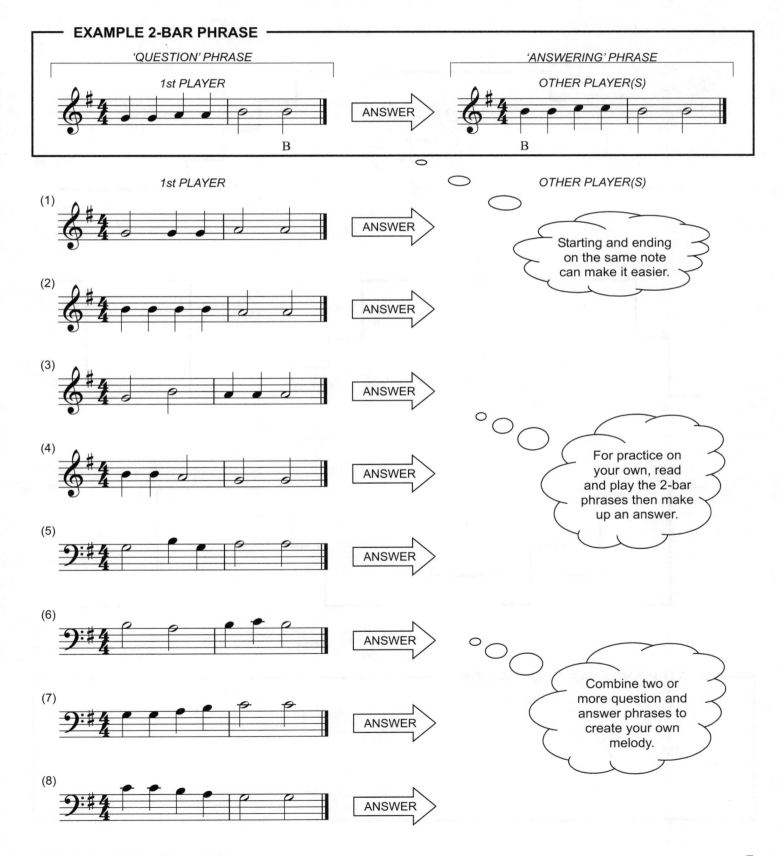

Pitch by Steps and Leaps

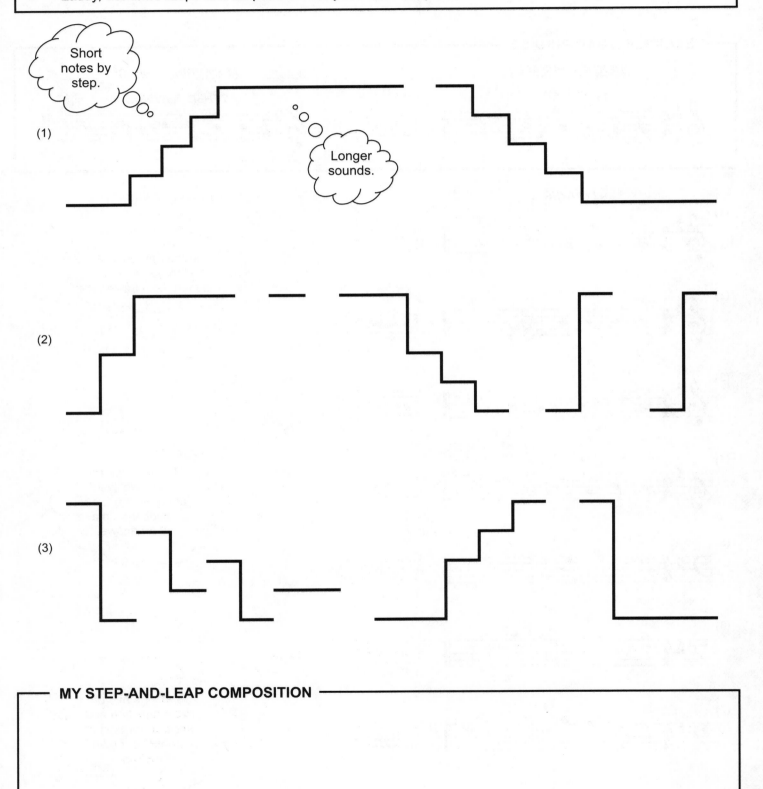

(1)

(2)

(3)

┌─ MY STEP-AND-LEAP COMPOSITION ─────────────────────────┐
│   │
│   │
│   │
│   │
│   │
│   │
└──┘

TWM00149

Play a Well-Known Tune 'By Ear'

Au Clair de la Lune *[CD09, CD10, CD11]*

G G G A B A (♩ ♩ ♩ ♩ o)

Merrily We Roll Along *[CD12, CD13, CD14]*

B A G A B B B (♩ ♩ ♩ ♩ ♩ ♩)

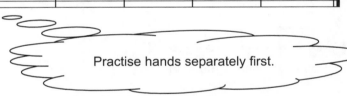

Practise hands separately first.

Memorising (1)

In the BAG!

B A G   B A G   A B C C B   B A G   B A G   A B C A G

Call a CAB!

C A B   C B A C B   C A B   C B A G A

Word-Rhythms

- This word-rhythm activity is for two or more players and is in 'G' position.
- Maintaining a 4- beat pulse, practise saying aloud and clapping each cartoon word-rhythm.
- Then, guided by the arrows, clap and say aloud each rhythm-pattern in turn. *[CD15]*
- Next, play the word-rhythms on your instrument on any note(s). *[CD15]*
- Lastly, play the word-rhythms drawing on notes from the arpeggio. *[CD16]*

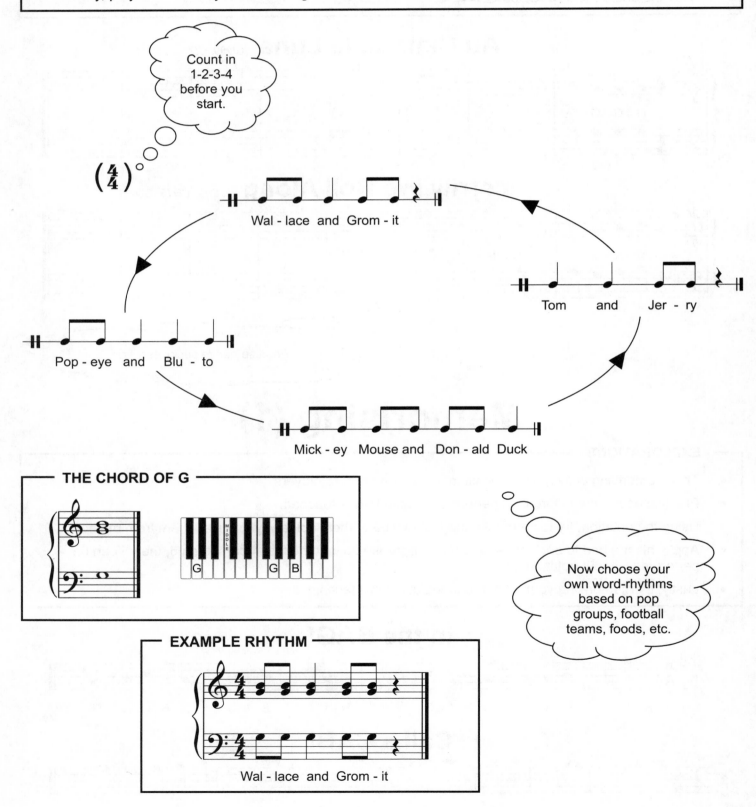

TWM00149   © Team World Music Ltd 2005

Rhythm Grids

Count in 1-2-3-4.

You can play a rhythm grid fast, slow, high, low, quiet or loud.

(1)

(2)

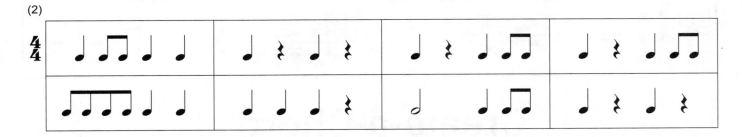

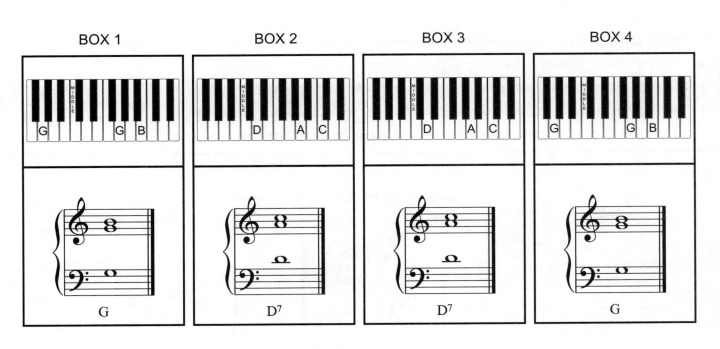

Staccato Starter

REPEATED CROTCHETS

THE CHORD

G

EXAMPLE RHYTHMS

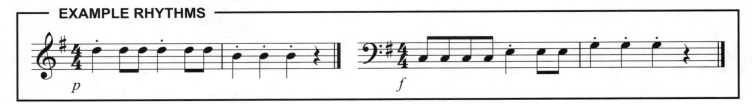

ACCOMPANIMENT

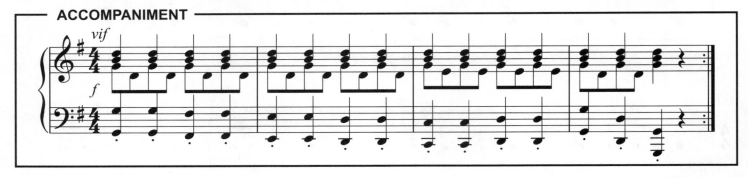

Create-a-Chord

EXAMPLE CHORD

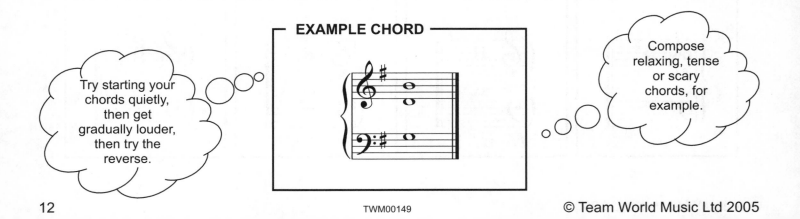

Try starting your chords quietly, then get gradually louder, then try the reverse.

Compose relaxing, tense or scary chords, for example.

TWM00149

Dot-Dash Phrases

- This activity is for one or more players.
- First, learn to play one of the given scales, with and without notation, as advised by your teacher.
- Starting on any note of the given scale, play the phrases by interpreting the dot-and-dash symbols (dots represent short sounds, and dashes represent long).
- Then perform 'Hopscotch' which combines dot-dash phrases.
- Lastly, using the given phrases and example titles below, compose your own piece of descriptive music. Notate your composition in the box provided.

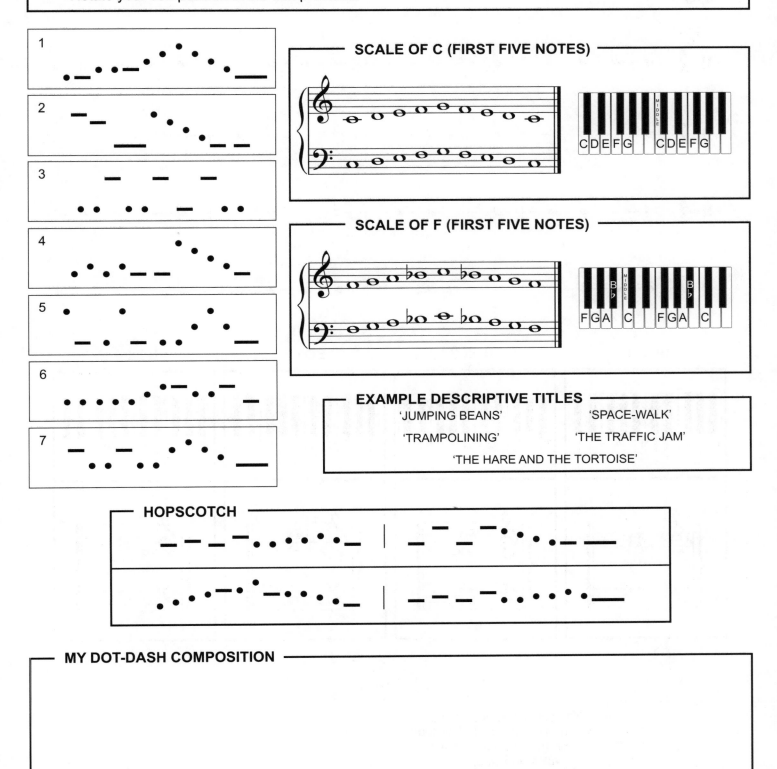

SCALE OF C (FIRST FIVE NOTES)

SCALE OF F (FIRST FIVE NOTES)

EXAMPLE DESCRIPTIVE TITLES

'JUMPING BEANS'   'SPACE-WALK'

'TRAMPOLINING'   'THE TRAFFIC JAM'

'THE HARE AND THE TORTOISE'

HOPSCOTCH

MY DOT-DASH COMPOSITION

TWM00149

A Rhythm Round

- This rhythm round, for two or more players, can be clapped, sung, or played in 'F' position.

- Practise the rhythm, then play it as a round or in unison, or in harmony using notes from the chord boxes below. *[CD19]* You may add words to the given rhythms.

- Each chord box lasts for one bar.

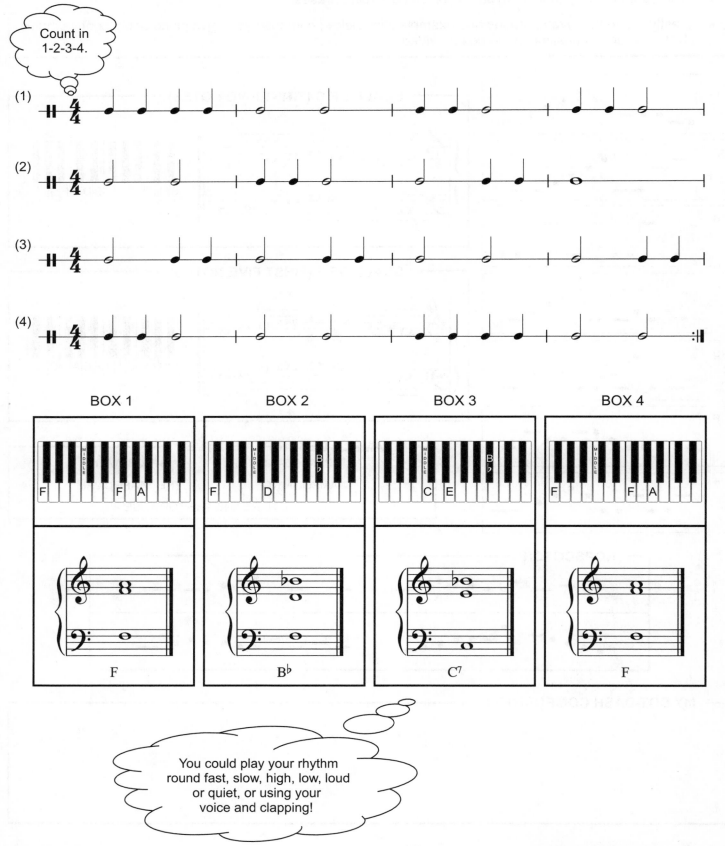

TWM00149

Matching Sound to Symbol

●	Short, loud sound	●	Short, quiet sound
▬▬▬	Long, loud sound	─────	Long, quiet sound
• • • •	Row of quiet short sounds	● ● ● ●	Row of loud short sounds
Three notes going upwards		Three notes going downwards	
An upward interval		A downward interval	
Two slurred notes close together		Two slurred notes wide apart	
(−) Short silence		(▬▬▬) Long silence	

GRAPHIC SCORE

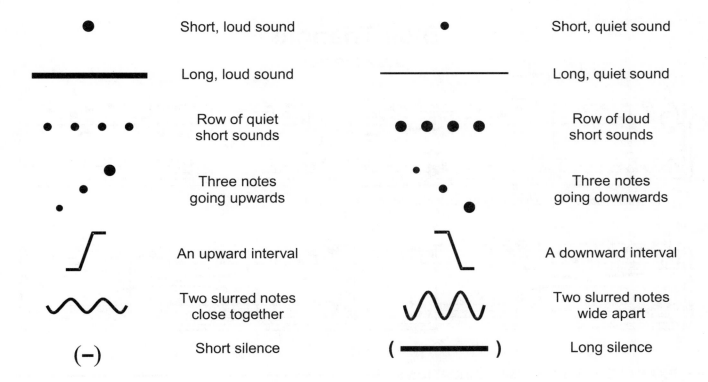

(1)

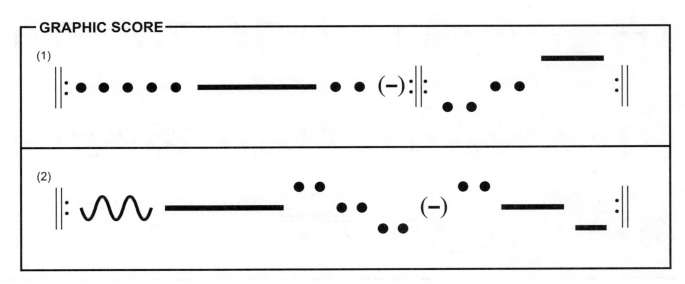

(2)

MY OWN COMPOSITION

Jazz on 3 Notes

Blue Triangle
(Jazz theme)

Medium swing tempo

(The middle note of each chord may be omitted to simplify, if required)

EXAMPLE 2- & 4-BAR IMPROVISATIONS

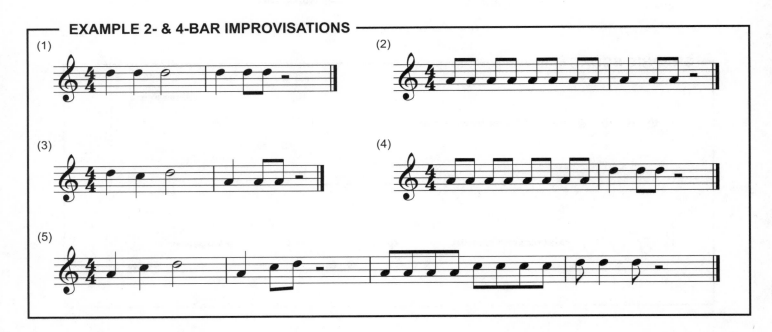

12-BAR BLUES ACCOMPANIMENT

D⁷	G⁷	D⁷	D⁷	G⁷	G⁷	D⁷	D⁷	Em⁷	A⁷	D⁷	D⁷

TWM00149

A Sound-Effect Story

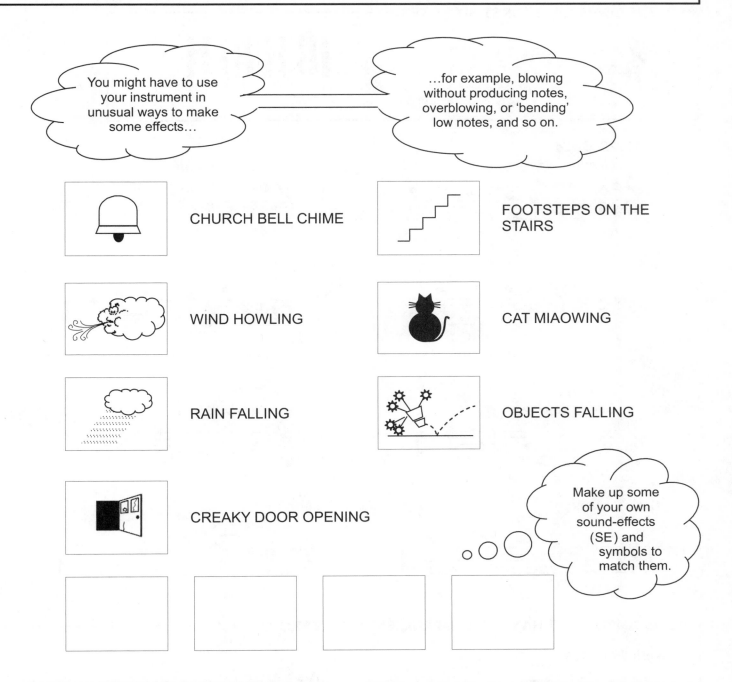

You might have to use your instrument in unusual ways to make some effects…

…for example, blowing without producing notes, overblowing, or 'bending' low notes, and so on.

CHURCH BELL CHIME

FOOTSTEPS ON THE STAIRS

WIND HOWLING

CAT MIAOWING

RAIN FALLING

OBJECTS FALLING

CREAKY DOOR OPENING

Make up some of your own sound-effects (SE) and symbols to match them.

EXAMPLE SOUND-EFFECT STORY

"I don't know why I went up to the old house that night. They said it was haunted, but I never believed them. But I must admit, I sure felt a bit uneasy that night.

The wind howled (SE). The rain lashed down (SE). And for some unknown reason, the church bell struck one (SE) even though it was only ten! Anyway, I…(etc)"

TWM00149

Listen, Copy and Answer (1)

EXPLORATIONS

- This listen, copy and answer activity, in the key of G, is for two or more players.
- Play each of the 2-bar phrases below. Each phrase should then be immediately copied or answered by another player. *[CD23 - 26]*
- The 'answering' phrases should use notes and rhythms from the question phrases.
- This activity can be performed using the example keyboard accompaniment. *[CD23 - 26]*

THE SCALE OF G (FIRST SIX NOTES)

G A B C D E

(1) *[CD23, CD24]*
Gently flowing

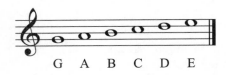

mf

(2)
Gently flowing

mf

(3)

mf

(4)

mf
(FOUR FURTHER 2-BAR EXAMPLES GIVEN ON CD)

(5) *[CD25, CD26]*
Gently flowing

mf

(6)
Gently flowing

mf

(7)

mf

(8)

mf
(FOUR FURTHER 2-BAR EXAMPLES GIVEN ON CD)

EXAMPLE LEFT HAND ACCOMPANIMENT AND IMPROVISATION

Gently Flowing

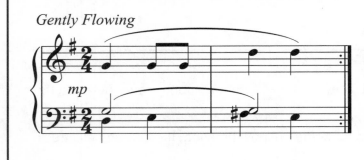

mp

TWM00149

Make Up a Song

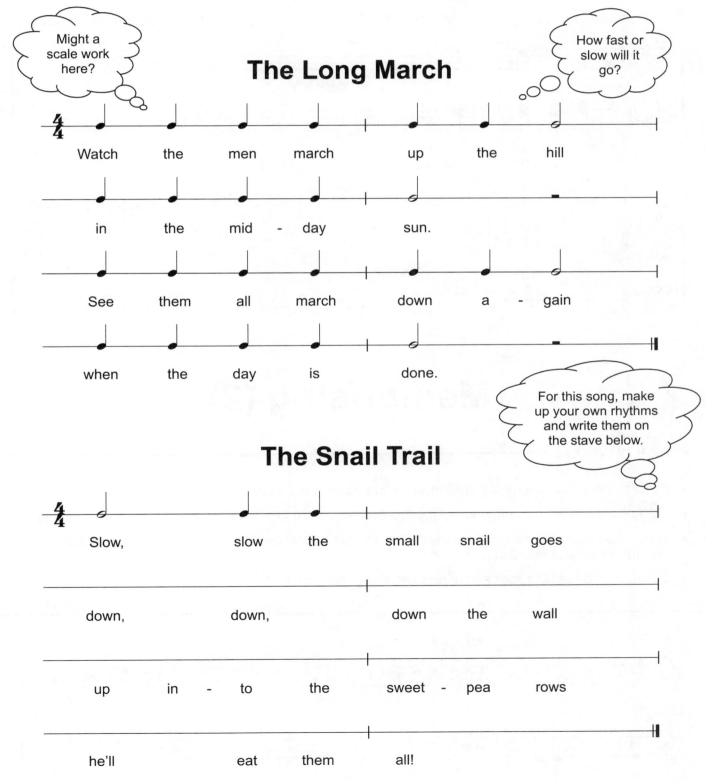

Name That Tune

EXPLORATIONS

- Taking each tune in turn, play or sing the 2-bar prompt and identify it.

- Then try to complete the melody 'by ear', listening carefully to whether each note is higher, lower, longer or shorter than the previous.

- Practise slowly and methodically, correcting mistakes, repeating phrases as appropriate, until you can play the entire melody. Then choose appropriate chords (from those given) to harmonise the melody.

- Once you have learned each melody, try to notate it in the bars provided. *[CD27 – CD32]*

Slowly   [CD27, CD28, CD29]

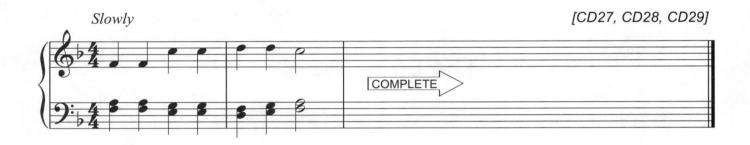

Quickly   [CD30, CD31, CD32]

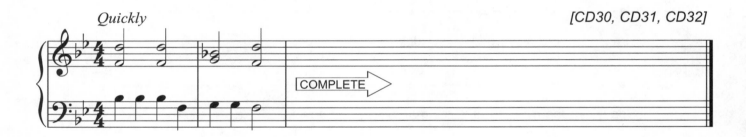

Memorising (2)

EXPLORATIONS

- Practise each line in turn until performance standard is reached.

- Using the notation, try to memorise the first two bars, then look away and play them from memory.

- Apply this method to each subsequent 2-bar phrase so that the first 4 bars, then 6, then 8 can be performed without notation.

- Lastly, try memorising your favourite tunes using this technique.

      TWM00149

Instant Ensemble

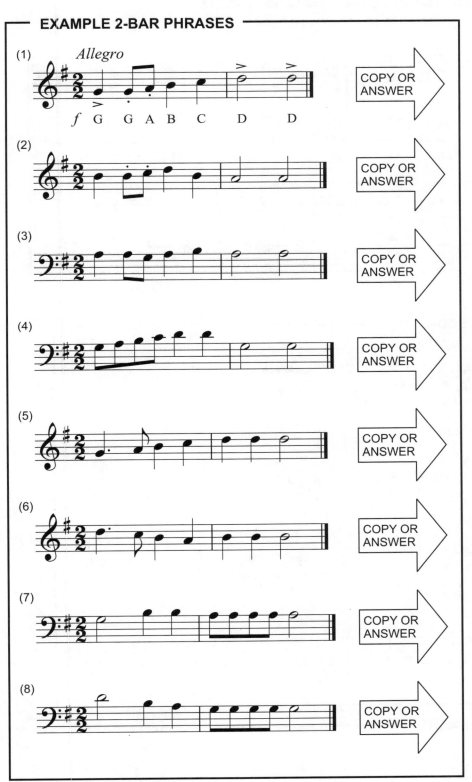

EXAMPLE 2-BAR PHRASES

(1) *Allegro*
f G G A B C D D

COPY OR ANSWER

(2) COPY OR ANSWER

(3) COPY OR ANSWER

(4) COPY OR ANSWER

(5) COPY OR ANSWER

(6) COPY OR ANSWER

(7) COPY OR ANSWER

(8) COPY OR ANSWER

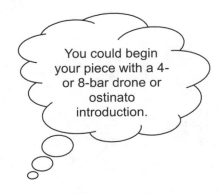

You could begin your piece with a 4- or 8-bar drone or ostinato introduction.

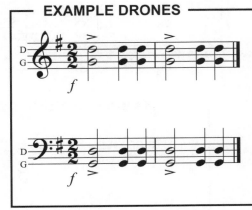

EXAMPLE DRONES

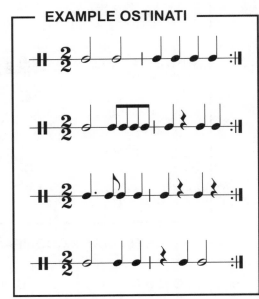

EXAMPLE OSTINATI

Rhythmic Decoration

EXPLORATIONS

- Learn to play 'Old MacDonald Had a Farm', in the key of G, individually or in a group. *[CD35]*
- Experiment decorating the rhythm, as shown in the examples, working two bars at a time. *[CD36 - 39]*
- Perform the piece using rhythmic decoration of your choice. *[CD36 - 39]*

Old MacDonald Had a Farm

EXAMPLE RHYTHMIC DECORATION

WITH REPEATED NOTES *[CD36]*	(1)
WITH JAZZ RHYTHMS *[CD37]*	(2)
WITH DECORATED LONG NOTES *[CD38]*	(3)
WITH A CHANGE OF TIME SIGNATURE *[CD39]*	(4)

KEYBOARD ACCOMPANIMENT

| G | C | G | G/D | D⁷ | G | G | C | G | G/D | D⁷ | G | G | G⁷ | C | Cm⁷ | G | C | G | G/D | D⁷ | G |

TWM00149

Melodic Decoration

EXPLORATIONS

- Learn to play 'Old MacDonald Had a Farm', in the key of G, individually or in a group. *[CD35]*

- Experiment decorating the pitch, as shown in the examples below, working two bars at a time. You may also need to consider rhythmic decoration. *[CD40 – 43]*

- Perform the piece using melodic (and rhythmic) decoration of your choice. *[CD40 – 43]*

Old MacDonald Had a Farm (Example 3 below)

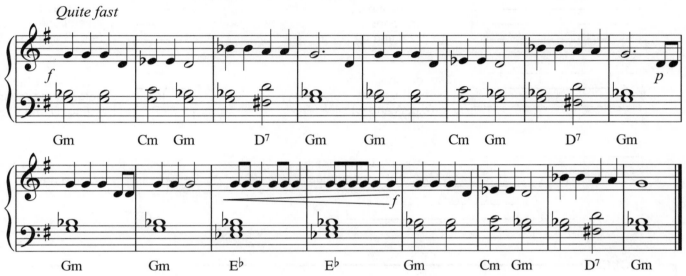

EXAMPLE PITCH (AND RHYTHMIC) DECORATION

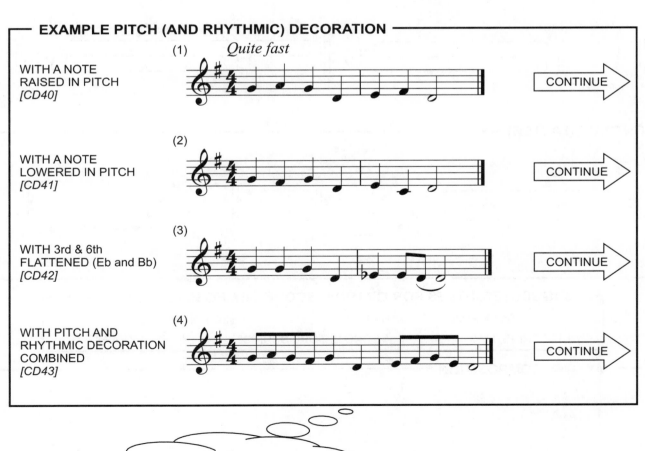

WITH A NOTE RAISED IN PITCH *[CD40]* — (1)

WITH A NOTE LOWERED IN PITCH *[CD41]* — (2)

WITH 3rd & 6th FLATTENED (Eb and Bb) *[CD42]* — (3)

WITH PITCH AND RHYTHMIC DECORATION COMBINED *[CD43]* — (4)

Now try decorating the pitch and rhythm of some of your favourite tunes.

TWM00149

Sound-Scape

EXPLORATIONS

- This activity gives further opportunity to interpret symbols creatively.

- In your group, using notes of your own choice, play through all the symbols below.

- Next, using a combination of these symbols, and those from 'Matching Sound to Symbol', find ways of interpreting 'Icicles'. You can use a selection of keyboard 'voices' for the various symbols.

- Finally, compose your own piece, notating it using the suggested symbols.

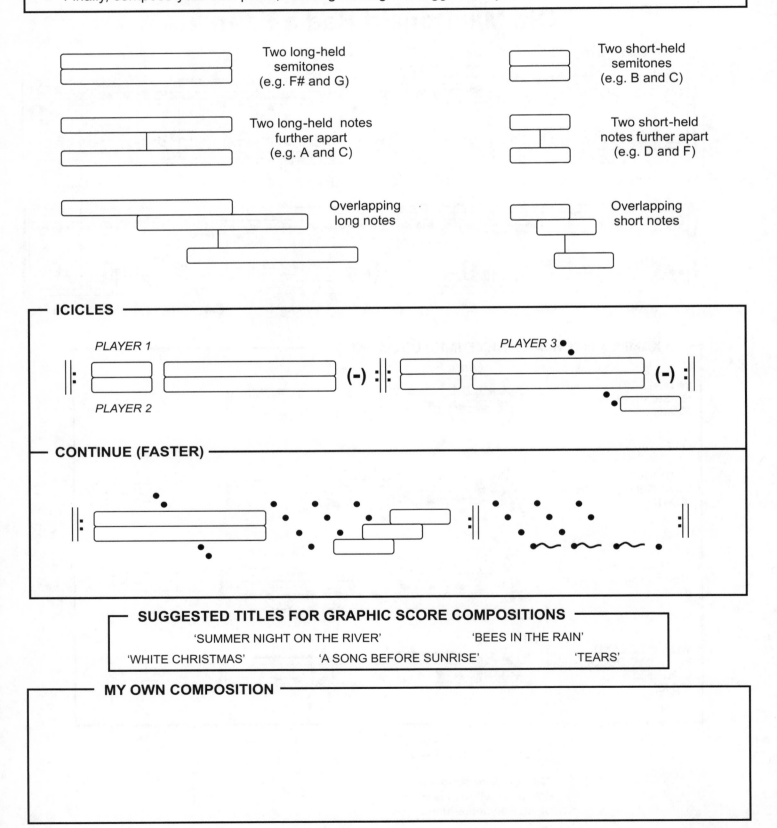

Two long-held semitones (e.g. F# and G)

Two short-held semitones (e.g. B and C)

Two long-held notes further apart (e.g. A and C)

Two short-held notes further apart (e.g. D and F)

Overlapping long notes

Overlapping short notes

ICICLES

PLAYER 1

PLAYER 3

PLAYER 2

(-)

(-)

CONTINUE (FASTER)

SUGGESTED TITLES FOR GRAPHIC SCORE COMPOSITIONS

'SUMMER NIGHT ON THE RIVER'   'BEES IN THE RAIN'

'WHITE CHRISTMAS'   'A SONG BEFORE SUNRISE'   'TEARS'

MY OWN COMPOSITION

TWM00149

Chinese Music

- This Chinese music activity, for one or more players, is based upon a pentatonic scale, in 'F' position.
- First, learn to play the pentatonic scale given, then practise 'Red Dragon'. *[CD44]*
- Next, experiment improvising 2- and 4-bar phrases based upon the scale. *[CD45]*
- Finally, perform 'Red Dragon', alternating the melody with improvised passages, and adding drone and ostinato accompaniment as indicated in the examples below. *[CD46]*

© Team World Music Ltd 2005   TWM00149   25

Composing with Copy and Answer

EXPLORATIONS

- In this activity you can learn how to compose an ending for an incomplete melody in G major.

- First, practise the given example in order to see how a 4-bar phrase can be 'answered' by a 4-bar phrase using the copy and answer technique.

- Then compose endings for each of the incomplete melodies below.

EXAMPLE COPY AND ANSWER TECHNIQUE

Composing with Mirror Technique

Try to sing an ending before you play it.

In 'Mirror Technique', the reflection does not have to be an exact mirror image.

Caribbean Rhythm Round

BOX 1   BOX 2

Each chord-box lasts for one bar.

C⁷   F⁶

KEYBOARD ACCOMPANIMENT

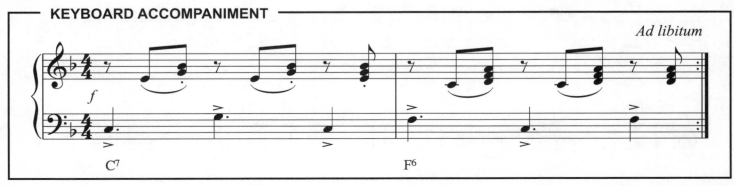

C⁷   F⁶

TWM00149

Blues Booster

Movin' On

BLUES SCALE ON 'A' (DOMINANT TO DOMINANT)

E G A B C D D♯ E

Medium Swing Tempo

(The middle note of each chord may be omitted to simplify, if required)

EXAMPLE 2- & 4-BAR IMPROVISATIONS

12-BAR BLUES ACCOMPANIMENT

A⁷	D⁷	A⁷	A⁷	D⁷	D⁷	A⁷	A⁷	Bm⁷	E⁷	D⁷	D⁷

TWM00149

Favourite Tunes 'By Ear'

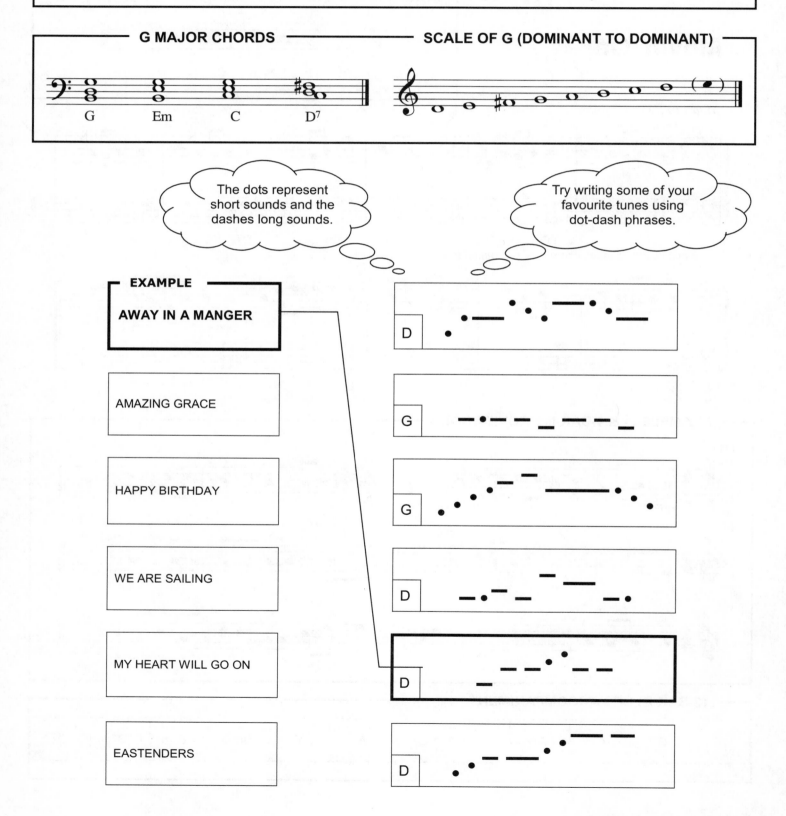

TWM00149

Whole-Tone Improvising

EXPLORATIONS

- This improvisation activity is for two or more players.

- First, learn and memorise the whole-tone scale of C.

- Practise playing the scale, both ascending and descending, using the example rhythms given. *[CD52]*

- Then, try improvising your own rhythm patterns and perform. *[CD52, CD53]*

- Lastly, improvise rhythm patterns to create a spooky, atmospheric composition. *[CD54]*

WHOLE-TONE SCALE OF C

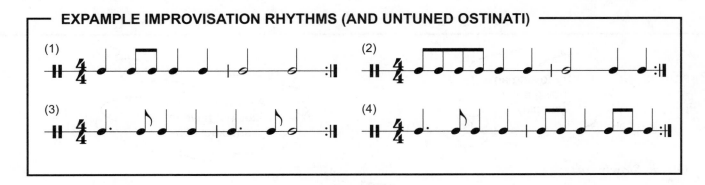

EXPAMPLE IMPROVISATION RHYTHMS (AND UNTUNED OSTINATI)

DRONE ACCOMPANIMENT

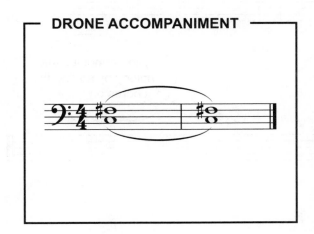

OSTINATI

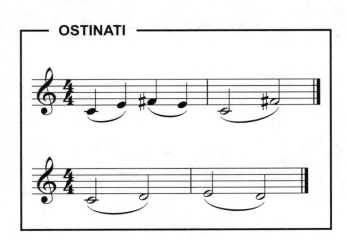

EXAMPLE OSTINATO PIANO ACCOMPANIMENT

TWM00149

Composing with Sequence

EXPLORATIONS

- In this activity you can learn how to compose an ending for an incomplete melody.

- First, practise the given examples in order to see how a phrase can be 'answered' by another phrase using sequence.

- Then, using this sequence technique, compose endings for each of the incomplete melodies below.

EXAMPLE SEQUENCE PHRASE TECHNIQUE

(1) (2) (3)

Try to sing an ending before you play it.

A sequence phrase does not have to be an exact copy.

(4) *Slowly*
p

Try to harmonise this melody by adding the chords on page 30.

(5) *Jolly*
f

(6) *Allegro*
mf

Now see if you can also complete these melodies by using 'Mirror Technique' or 'Copy and Answer'.

TWM00149 © Team World Music Ltd 2005

Listen, Copy and Answer (2)

EXPLORATIONS

- This listen, copy and answer activity is for two or more players.

- First, learn to play 'Echo Mountain' and perform it twice through with a chordal accompaniment. *[CD55]*

- Next, in your group, practise copying each 2-bar phrase as indicated in the given example *[CD56]*. Then experiment answering each 2-bar phrase with a 2-bar improvisation, as illustrated below. *[CD57]*

- Finally, perform 'Echo Mountain' incorporating copied or answering phrases. *[CD57]*

Echo Mountain

EXAMPLE COPIED PHRASE

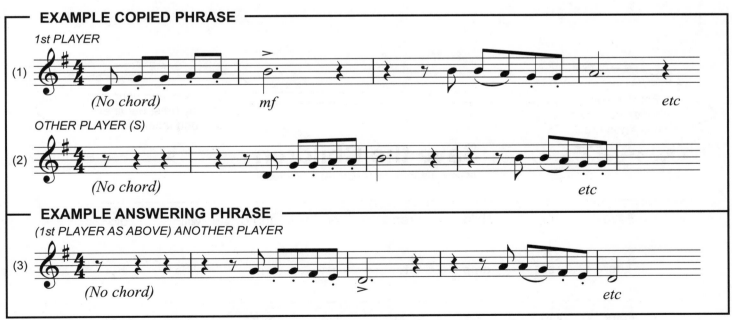

KEYBOARD ACCOMPANIMENT

G	G	D	D	Am^7	D^7	G	G^7	C	C	G	Em	Am	D^7	G	G

TWM00149

Songs of Persuasion

Copy-Cat

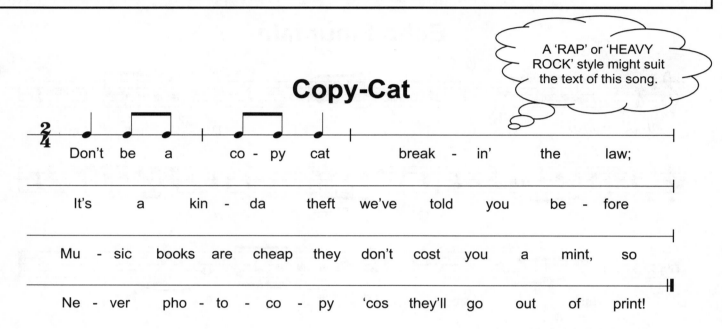

A 'RAP' or 'HEAVY ROCK' style might suit the text of this song.

Don't	be	a	co - py	cat	break - in'	the	law;
It's	a	kin - da	theft	we've	told	you	be - fore
Mu - sic	books	are cheap	they	don't	cost	you	a mint, so
Ne - ver	pho - to - co - py	'cos	they'll	go	out	of	print!

For this song, choose your own time-signature…

…now add your own rhythms, bar lines, and letter-names.

Save the Children

[Words and Music by 10-year old Sian Hindle]

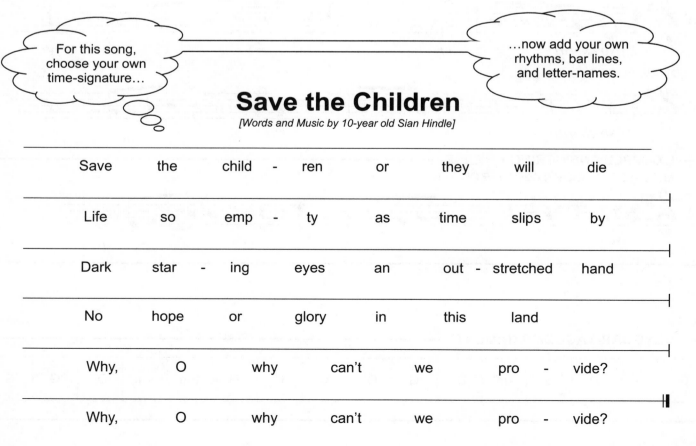

Save	the	child - ren	or	they	will	die
Life	so	emp - ty	as	time	slips	by
Dark	star - ing	eyes	an	out - stretched	hand
No	hope	or	glory	in	this	land
Why,	O	why	can't	we	pro - vide?
Why,	O	why	can't	we	pro - vide?

TWM00149

Tell a Story with Music

- This descriptive music activity is for two or more players.

- Read through each story and choose one to illustrate with music.

- Then, using a variety of 'voices', experiment with scale and arpeggio patterns and sound effects to describe the actions in the text.

- Lastly, perform your story with music, with or without a narrator.

PARACHUTISTS

You are in the park during a Spring festival. You look up and see three parachutists coming down towards you. They seem to fall slowly at first, spiralling round and around, but as they get lower they appear to be falling faster. The first parachutist lands heavily just a few metres from where you are. The second one disappears behind some trees. The third one gets it all wrong and lands in the lake!

BONFIRE NIGHT

It's Bonfire Night and someone lights three rockets. The fuse on the first one burns for a few seconds, then the rocket flies up very quickly and bursts into colour. The second one is damp and only manages to fly up slowly to about twenty metres before it explodes. The third rocket is damaged; it rises to a metre and flies round and round the garden out of control and smashes into a window.

THE HARE AND THE TORTOISE

The hare and the tortoise agree to have a race. Off goes the starting gun! The hare leaps forward at almighty speed; the tortoise, plodding along, is left behind. Far ahead of the tortoise, the hare decides to take a break and drifts off to sleep. The tortoise continues to plod forward, but eventually overtakes the sleeping hare. At the last minute, the hare awakes. Aware of his mistake, he rushes towards the finishing line. But it is too late, the tortoise ambles across the line and wins the race.

JOURNEY INTO SPACE

5, 4, 3, 2, 1... the rockets are ignited and the shuttle blasts upwards towards the sky. Soon the craft reaches the stratosphere, and enters outer space. The shuttle cruises through space and time, beyond the known planets. Months pass, and the crew reach their destination, landing on a strange and bizarre world. Contact is made with alien creatures...

You could notate your story-with-music using a graphic score.

EXAMPLE - STORY 1

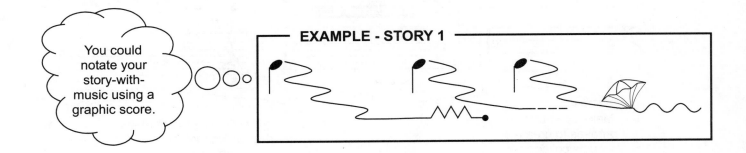

Sound Collage

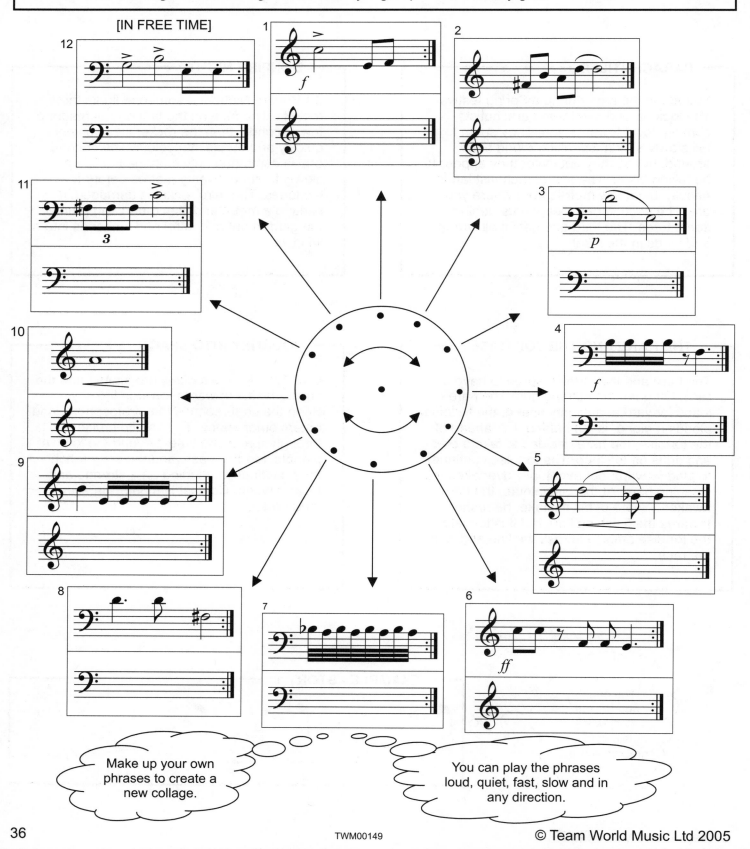

Salsa Rhythm Round

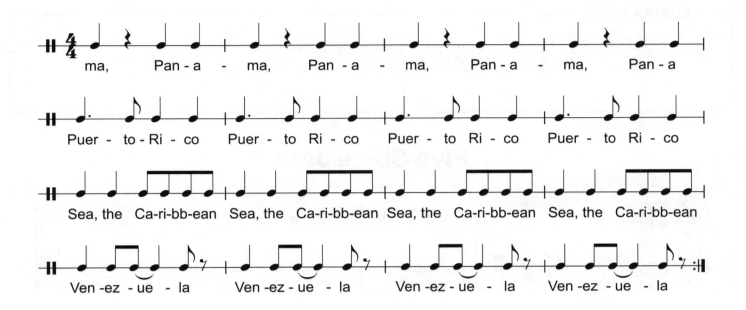

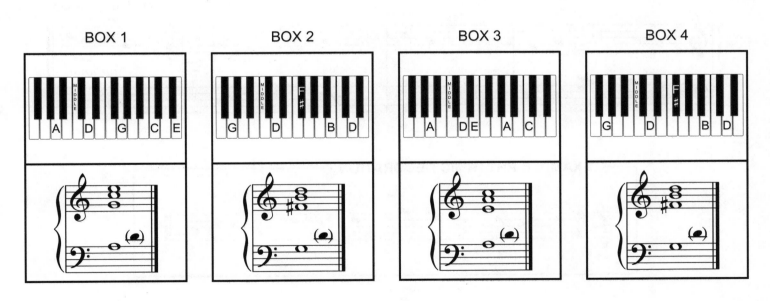

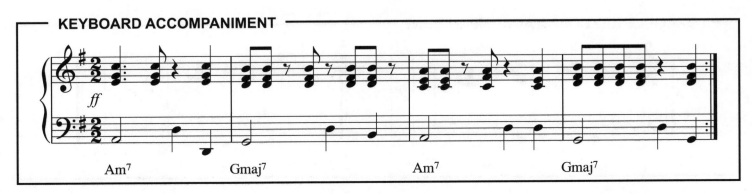

TWM00149

Dorian Jazz

DORIAN MODE

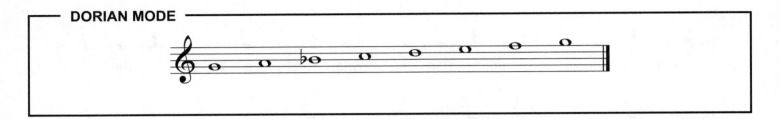

Five Spice Jazz

EXAMPLE RHYTHMIC DECORATION

EXAMPLE KEYBOARD ACCOMPANIMENT

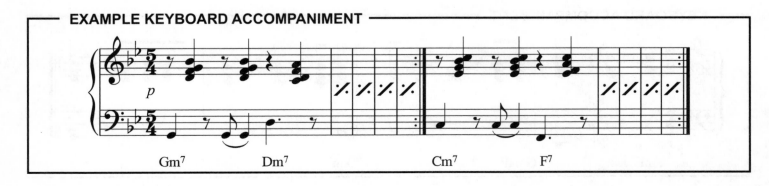

Gm⁷   Dm⁷   Cm⁷   F⁷

TWM00149

Composing Descriptive Music

EXAMPLE TITLES

'MOONWALK'   'LULLABY'

'CHINA TOWN'   'SLEIGH RIDE'

'CARIBBEAN STREET PARTY'

'SEA SCAPE'   'THE ELEPHANT'

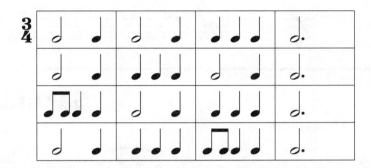

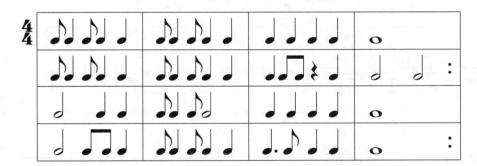

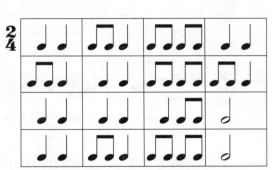

SCALE OF F MAJOR

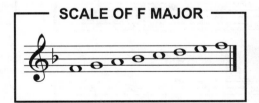

PENTATONIC SCALE

WHOLE-TONE SCALE OF C

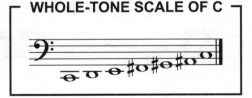

EXAMPLE STARTING POINTS

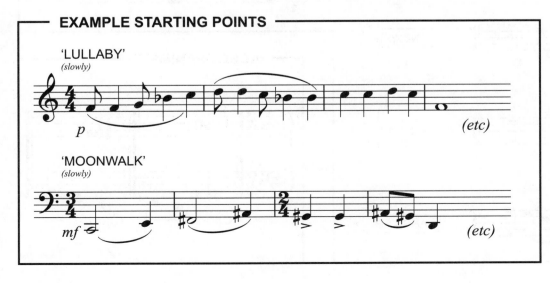

'LULLABY'
(slowly)

'MOONWALK'
(slowly)

Now make up your own list of descriptive titles and compose another piece of music.

Japanese Music

EXPLORATIONS

- This Japanese music activity is for one or more players.

- First, learn to play the Japanese 'In' Scale with its differing ascending and descending pattern, then practise 'Sakura'. *[CD65]*. Another player can learn to play the given accompaniment.

- Next, experiment answering 2-bar phrases with 2-bar improvisations, as in the examples below, with accompaniment. *[CD66]*

- Finally, perform 'Sakura', alternating the melody with improvised passages. *[CD67]*

JAPANESE 'IN' SCALE

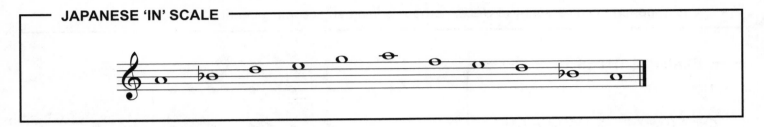

Sakura

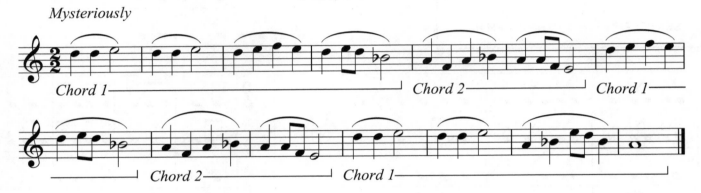

EXAMPLE 2-BAR QUESTION AND ANSWER PHRASES

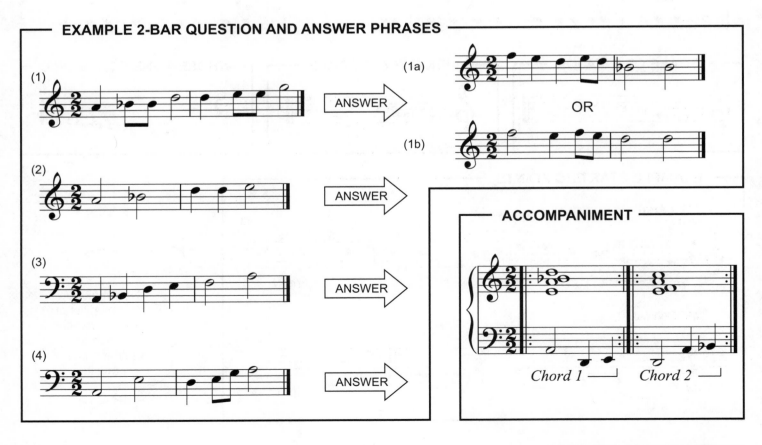

TWM00149

Minimalism

- This minimalism activity is for three or more players.

- Each player chooses one of the given 4-bar ostinati and at an agreed moment changes to a different ostinato part. *[CD68]*. A selection of keyboard 'voices' can be used for each phrase.

- In boxes 7 and 8, compose your own ostinato which can be performed with the composition. Use rhythms of your choice and draw from the notes given below. *[CD68]*

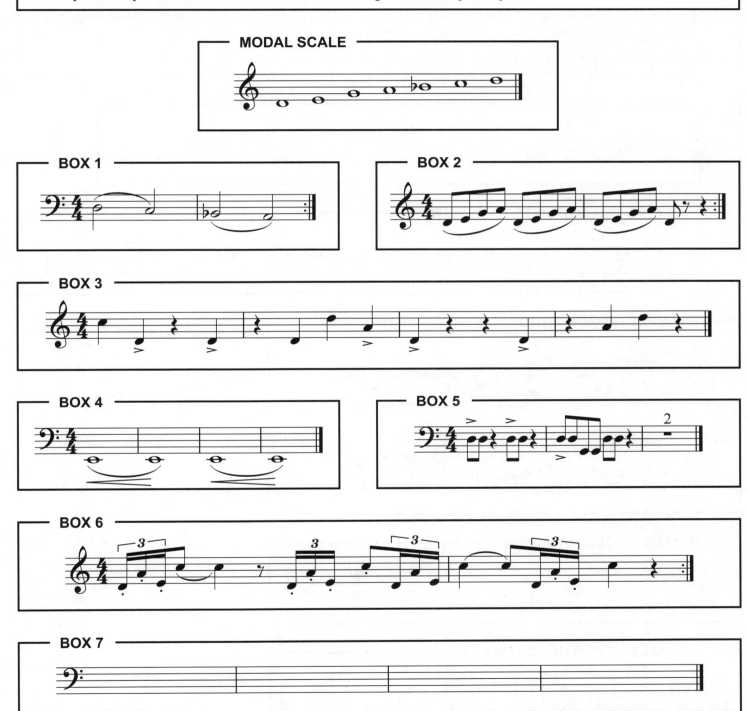

TWM00149

Dodecaphonic Music

TONE-ROW

RETROGRADE TONE-ROW

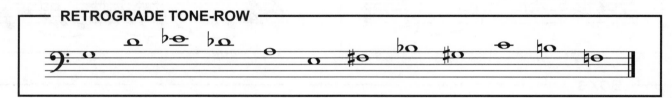

EXAMPLE IMPROVISATIONS

You can play your improvisation in 'strict' or 'free' time.

EXAMPLE ACCOMPANIMENT

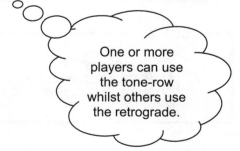

One or more players can use the tone-row whilst others use the retrograde.

EXAMPLE KEYBOARD OSTINATO

Try starting your improvisation at different points in the row.

TWM00149

Improvising with Ragas

EXPLORATIONS

- This composing ragas activity is for two or more players.
- First, learn to play the raga ascending and descending, and then memorise it. *[CD70]*
- Next, take turns to improvise 2-bar phrases as in the examples below. Then add the accompaniment. *[CD71]*
- Lastly, compose your own raga based on your improvisations, and perform it, adding the example drones and an ostinato. *[CD71]*

THE RAGA

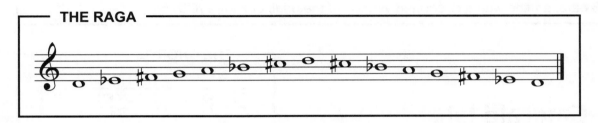

EXAMPLE 2-BAR PHRASES

EXAMPLE DRONE AND OSTINATO

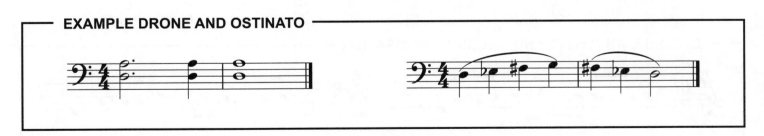

KEYBOARD ACCOMPANIMENT

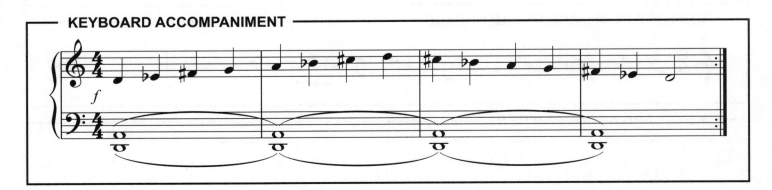

     TWM00149

Jigs and Reels

THE CHORDS

Emerald Isle

EXAMPLE RHYTHMIC AND MELODIC DECORATION

EXAMPLE IMPROVISED 4-BAR PHRASE

KEYBOARD ACCOMPANIMENT

Am	G	Am	G	Am	Em	Am Em	Am	C	G	Am	Em	Am Em	Am G	Am Em	Am

TWM00149

'C' Position Activities

(No CD tracks available)

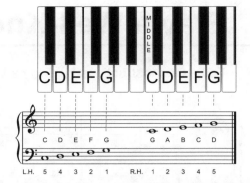

Listen and Copy

- Follow the instructions for 'Listen and Copy' on page 6.
- EXAMPLES:

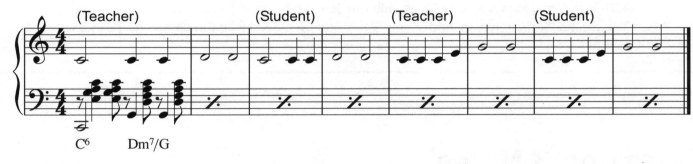

- Gradually introduce C, D, E, F and G.
- Develop also left hand responses and then both hands together.

Listen and Answer

- Follow the instructions for 'Listen and Answer' on page 7.
- EXAMPLES:

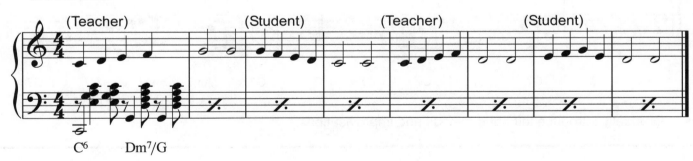

- Develop also left hand responses and then both hands together.

Memorising

- Follow the instructions for 'Memorising' on page 9.

'EGG for Tea!'

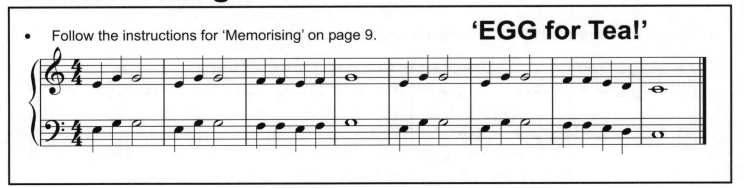

Play a Well-Known Tune 'By Ear'

- Follow the instructions for 'Play a Well-Known Tune 'By Ear'' on page 9.

- 'Merrily We Roll Along' can also be played with the Teachers' accompaniment.
- 'When The Saints Go Marchin' In' and 'Jingle Bells' can be played with the same chords in a re-ordered sequence.

Jazz on 3 Notes

- Follow the instructions for 'Jazz on 3 Notes' on page 16.

- Gradually introduce left hand melody and improvisations.

Composing with Copy and Answer

- Follow the instructions for 'Composing with Copy and Answer' on page 26.

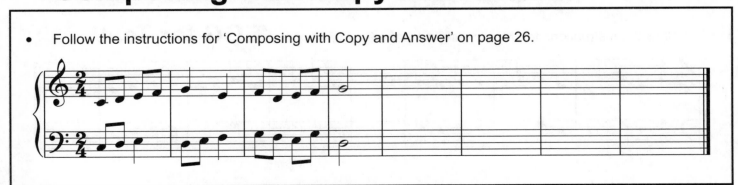